Sometimes I'm gentle.

Feathery flakes float from the sky
to frost branches and rooftops
or vanish on your tongue.

I draw lacy patterns on windowpanes and softly *whoosh* drifts into astonishing shapes.

Know where I can find a teeny tiny hat?

I am Winter,
season of cold and snow.

Open spaces sparkle
in the sun and glitter
purple-blue under
the stars.

Other times I'm stormy.

Stinging needles of sleet and howling
arctic blasts set little birds trembling.

Rabbits and squirrels,
take cover!

Brrr.

When it's not *too* cold, come and play!

Feel free to flap an angel or roll a jolly snowman.

Flop onto a sled and slip-slide down a bumpy hill. Hold tight!

My days are short.
    Darkness falls early.

Ever skimmed outdoor ice
on silver blades?

Click-clack-click.
    Can't do *that* in the summertime!

I am Winter,
keeper of your
favorite holidays.

Twinkle lights and colorful displays cheer neighbors and friends.

Festive meals invite visitors to gather around the table.

You might exchange gifts around a merry tree and sing carols of the season.

You might listen to family stories and honor age-old traditions that help you remember the past.

When the year fades away, you can count on me to supply a new one.

Celebrate!

I am sneaky.

About the time you think I'll never go away, I send a soft, warm day to make icicles drip and snowbanks melt into shallow puddles.

Still,
I might *zap* you with
one last blizzard, just for kicks.

I'll leave—for a while.
But when the year nears its end,
watch for my return.

Will I be gentle or stormy,
playful or sneaky? Wait and see.